WILL SUCCESS SPOIL JEFF DAVIS?

WILL SUCCESS SPOIL JEFF DAVIS?

The Last Book About
THE CIVIL WAR

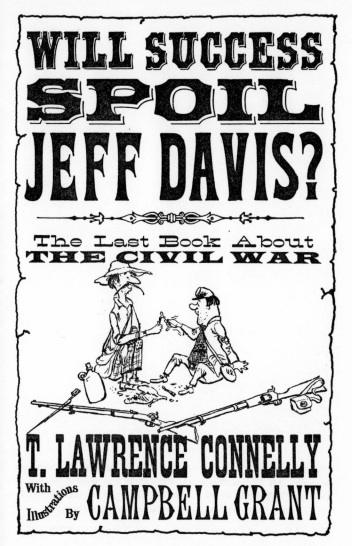

T. LAWRENCE CONNELLY

With Illustrations By **CAMPBELL GRANT**

McGRAW-HILL BOOK COMPANY, INC.

NEW YORK TORONTO LONDON

Contents

———◆———

To my wife, Sally Evelyn,

who gave me the ideas . . .

wrote most of the manuscript . . .

typed the drafts . . .

corrected my errors . . .

changed the typewriter ribbon faithfully . . .

and most important—

laughed when it was not funny.

———◆———

The Professional Confederate

Confederatesmanship—The Professional Confederate

For more than ninety years, writers have peered through the battle smoke to catch a glimpse of that vanishing figure in gray—the Confederate. Alas, the old Confederate is no longer a hero to little boys in the corner drugstore. A host of writers have brought him into the average American home with a shocking degree of intimacy. Instead of reading about ghostly figures in gray topping Cemetery Ridge, we now are exposed to oversized accounts of everything from the degree of Confederate sinus drainage to Robert E. Lee's hair tonic. A new figure, who never was closer to the War than a Military Park tour, has risen to place his name alongside other great American folk types such as the lumberjack, the pioneer, the cowboy—the professional Confederate. Confederatesmanship is not a hobby ... it is a vocation. Almost anyone can be an *amateur* Confederate, for the qualifications are relatively easy to meet. Six out of ten of the following will make you an amateur and start you on the road to graydom:

1. Cry during *Gone with the Wind* (especially when the Yankees burn the Atlanta depot).
2. Own an LP album of Civil War songs.
3. Visit Gettysburg and buy a souvenir minié ball.
4. Yell like heck when someone raises a Rebel flag at a football game or a political rally.
5. Buy a copy of Freeman's *R. E. Lee* (worth three points).
6. Own a great-grandfather who rode with Jeb Stuart.
7. If you cannot qualify under number six, then have a great-grandmother who buried silver under the smokehouse.
8. Tell about your family plantation burned by Sherman's raiders. Grit your teeth when you say "Sherman" and challenge onlookers to sing "Marching through Georgia."
9. Own a piece of Confederate money.
10. Hate Jefferson Davis.

On the other hand, the professional Confederate, the ultimate of Confederatesmanship, is of an elite and highly classified group. He operates everywhere ... bars, hotel lobbies, cocktail parties. He may wear

Confederate socks, a Confederate tie, belt buckle, tie clasp, cuff links, and carry a cigarette lighter that plays "Dixie." However, his most distinguishing feature is his conversation. After only a few minutes a professional Confederate is identifiable as one of several types within the species.

1. *The Decisive Battler.* This type is one to be avoided at cocktail parties, for he is probably the most obnoxious and outspoken genus of the Confederates. Thoroughly convinced that the War was lost at *his* favorite battle, he refuses to associate with anyone but those who concur; as a result, current Civil War historians are divided into Pea Ridge School, Gettysburg School, *ad infinitum.*

2. *The Regimental Historian.* This second type of Confederate is easily spotted at any gathering. His hands are full of old muster rolls and glossy prints of regimental officers. To all Civil War writers he is the proverbial thorn. He constantly besieges them with letters of protest regarding minute errors in their writing. Colonel Blowhard, for example, belonged to the 45th Tennessee ... not the 44th. A sadist at heart, this Confederate's favorite game is to inform grief-stricken United Daughters of the Confederacy that their grandfathers' Tennessee regiment never served with Bedford Forrest ... the ultimate blow to the sirens in gray.

3. *The Ballistics Expert.* This Confederate is one of the angry young men of the new Southern army. Although his tour of duty never took him further than the Fort Benning Rifle Range, he sees himself as a Frederick the Great in butternut, convinced that the technical aspects of firearms is the *only* subject worthy of conversation. He thrills audiences with sulphurous accounts of the use of repeating rifles by Casement's division at the battle of Franklin, Tennessee, and waxes eloquent on such subjects as the slash marks on a Springfield rifle barrel and what might have happened if the North had used repeaters during the entire War. His home is usually armed like the Berlin frontier, with cannon balls, bayonets, and sabers. The most prized possession is always a Navy Colt carried by Jeb Stuart (of which there are only

fifty thousand in existence). His personal character-
istics: can lecture two hours on Patton's firepower on
the Rhine front . . . usually is missing several toes . . .
is often divorced.

4. *The Professional Kentuckian.* A rare and vanishing breed, the Kentuckians' stringed ties and Jeff
Davis beards are fast disappearing to the frozen
chicken pot pie industry. Usually a native of New
York City, the Professional Kentuckian is a frustrated would-be citizen of the state. The closest he
has been to the Bluegrass is *My Friend Flicka.* Yet
his eyes dim when someone plays "My Old Kentucky
Home"; he speaks softly of Churchill Downs, though
he is allergic to horses. He can establish kin with
everyone from Henry Clay to Man o' War. The fact
that little excitement happened in Kentucky during
the War (except a big Federal hog swindle in 1864)

does not diminish his pride. He goes berserk when someone suggests that John Morgan was an inept cavalryman, and babbles for hours over the excellence of Kentucky bourbon.

5. *The Antiquarian.* This Confederate is one of the most common types and spends most of his time prowling old attics and privies for war relics. The pack rat of the Confederacy, he collects anything that was around during the War and some things that were not. His home looks like the British Museum and smells like a quartermaster's warehouse. Where else could anyone find a six foot square print of the burial of Stonewall Jackson?

The collector is sometimes duped, however. For years northbound travelers on busy Highway 41 which follows the winding Tennessee River north from Chattanooga have stopped at a shabby house which bears the sign BATTLEFIELD SUVINERS CHEEP HEAR. They shell out for battered minié balls sold by a local rustic complete with stringed tie and "Y'all come." Several years ago, this rustic, who never got closer to the Chattanooga battlefields than a riverfront pool hall, confided his secret to me. Near the river bank is his workshop, complete with bullet mould and musket, and a garden of lead balls which are planted and harvested every year to be sold to Northern tourists. "They whupped us on the mountain but I'm getting 'em back now," he chuckled. And he is.

6. *The Nonprofessional Professional Virginian.* Usually a resident of Baltimore, Maryland, this Confederate's only connection with the Tidewater is frozen shrimp cocktail. Yet he readily hauls out his great-grandfather's uniform, which smells like a rejected Smithfield ham, and lectures on the "real waah." For him, there was no other general than "Bobby Lee" and no other army in the field than the Army of "Nawthun" Virginia.

7. *The Retired Army Officer.* This Confederate only makes his listeners wish that warfare had inflicted at least one more casualty. For some reason, the retired army officers are usually called Colonel and always have double last names. Most of them never rose higher than honorary captains in the Na-

tional Guard. Strategy and tactics are their cup of tea. They lecture for hours on what if Longstreet had and what if Stonewall Jackson had not. Other pastimes of this genus include collecting lead soldiers, wearing shabby tweed jackets, and damning Field Marshall Montgomery.

8. *The Genealogist*. These walking pension records are usually members of the Daughters of, and represent the elite of Confederatesmanship. Their motto is "Every man (especially my grandfather) his own slaveholder." No genealogist has yet existed who does not claim for his ancestors fifty slaves and a Tennessee valley plantation. They dominate conventions with sketches of the family history of General Beauregard. A most remarkable breed, they can by means of "research" (i.e., a five dollar bribe to the state archivist), transfer any inept private in their family into a Stonewall Jackson. Moreover, they can smell a battlefield site within fifty miles and determine if it is suitable for a historical marker. Many a site of a minor battle such as Dog Walk, Kentucky, is adorned with a massive half million dollar marble statue of Southern womanhood weeping over the wounded form of a Confederate. At least, the local birds are grateful.

9. *The Civil War Author*. Currently, the most popular Confederate is the Civil War author. One popular type of writer is the graduate student. Lord knows what the reading public would do without the

highly specialized Civil War students that the graduate mills grind out. Consider a few recent disserta-
tions, which unfortunately are often published in
book form:

"Saddle Soap Usage in Southwestern Virginia,
1861–1865."

"Confederate Hymn Book Production in East
Mississippi."

"An Inquiry into the Rate of Artillery Production
at Soakum Springs, Alabama: A Study of Company
Receipts and Deposits."

Not to be outdone, a new school of graduate in-
structors (labeled "literary historians") stress upon
their students writing style rather than technicality
and have produced such memorable works as "Fairy
Queene Symbols in the Career of Ben Butler."

A second source is the University Press, the sole
purpose of which is to publish the dull narratives of
Ph.D.'s that would not receive consideration else-
where. Almost every university press has a Civil War
centennial series. For example, recent publications
are:

*Journal of Ezra Snoot, Georgia Planter, 1864–
1865.*

*Civil War Letters of Private Humbert Blump,
46th Arkansas Infantry.*

*On to Richmond: the Journal of Emma Walnut,
Mascot, 1st Pennsylvania Bulgarian Zouaves.*

Children's books have not escaped the craze. The

old favorites have been conscripted and revised for quick sales. For example:

Born to Command: The Biography of Uncle Wiggley.

The Wizard of Oz and the Coming of the Civil War.

Tiny Tim and the Orphan Brigade.

Alice in Wonderland: The Military Strategy of Jefferson Davis.

The easiest way to publish something on the War is to submit an article to a historical journal. Better still, start your own journal. There are some two thousand in print and, judging by the tone of the articles, many of them are in need of material. Journal writing has its advantages. If he cannot write good prose, the writer can bury himself in footnotes. The footnote is a clever device, designed to confuse the general reader and absolve the author of any lawsuits. For example, consider a typical footnote to the statement "General Crumbley was a bastard." [34]

34. *Ibid.* see also, Cornstalk, *Bastards in Gray, loc. sic., op. sit., loc. site, sob.* Many maintain that General Crumbley was not a bastard. See *Thirty Years' View* by Mrs. Crumbley, *op. sit., sic. hoc.* Major Rumpley maintained that the General may have been a bastard but that he was indeed a "magnificent old bastard at that." See diary of Isaac Rumpley, Moose University Archives, XXCI, pt. 2, Sept. 21, 1863. In addition to being a bastard, the General was also a Mason. See diary of Cornelius Kraut, 1st Wisconsin Infantry, SWMVHR (XXI, Je. 45).

Closely akin to the article is that bit of academic payola, the book review. Reviews are written for three reasons—the reviewer needs a free copy of the book, the author is his worst enemy, or the author is his brother. Consequently, Civil War reviewers have developed their own language, which scarcely reveals what they are thinking. Consider a typical review:

"This is a very controversial book [*isn't worth a darn*]. It will probably evoke much comment [*still isn't worth a darn*]. Professor Klutch has a long-established career as a historian [*so why didn't he quit while he was ahead?*]. His biography of this great Confederate bastion [*bastard*], General Lost-cause, is one of several recent studies on this general [*fifty-three, to be exact*]. The book could stand a few minor corrections [*such as adding a bibliography, index, and notes*]. Despite a few technical errors [*it was the South that lost the War*], this volume is another creditable publication of Bellweather University Press [*they publish my book next week*].

The paperback trade has entered the competition for Civil War publications. Gory and lurid covers in your corner drugstore advertise the latest War novels.

Lady Chatterley's Forage Master.

Exodus—A Novel of Bragg's Military Career.

Look Backward, Angel—A Novel of the U.D.C.

A World I Never Made—A Brief History of the South.

The ultimate in Civil War bibliography is still the monograph. Several thousand are published each year, but only the top sellers can be mentioned here.

General E. J. Stackhouse. *Seeking the Lost: The Wilderness Campaign.*

Gunpowder Vandiver. *Mighty Stonewall: A Survey of Ante-Bellum Virginia Architecture.*

Gunpowder Vandiver. *Rebel Blast: A History of Confederate Ordnance.*

Clifford Dawdey. *The Land They Fought For: A History of White Citizens' Councils.*

Bull Wiley. *Farewell to Arms: The Life of Johnny Reb.*

Douglas Southall Freeholder. *I'll Cry Tomorrow: A Biography of R. E. Lee.*

Among the books not to include on your selected reading list are:

The Life and Sermons of Reverend Elijah Gooch of the 23rd Alabama Infantry in Six Volumes.

An Examination of the Techniques of Confederate Gunpowder Measuring with an Additional Report on Metallurgy Experiments Conducted at Relishburg, Georgia, Regarding the Density of Number Two Ironplate Cartridge Boxes, 1861– 1865.

Confederate Memorial Volume of Songs and Poems by Miss Cypress Pantaloon of Oxford, Mississippi, Together with the Funeral Orations of General Leonidas Polk.

History of the Forty-Third Arkansas Regiment, as Told by Its Old Commander; Appended to a Complete Roster of the Old Forty-Third.

The Complete Papers, Letters and Speeches of General Theophilus Holmes in Twenty-Seven Volumes.

How long will Confederatesmanship flourish? The new Confederacy receives reinforcements every year. The Long-Playing Record Collector has also joined the ranks. Time was when the only Civil War music available was either old movie soundtracks or ancient records of Roy Acuff singing "Battle Hymn of the Republic." Nowadays, Confederates gather and weep over a variety of albums. Every recording artist and some that are not have recorded Civil War albums. Some of the most notable ones are:

Songs I Wish I Could Have Sung the First Time Around, by the U.D.C. Chorale. This album includes such hits as "Marching through New York," and "Confederate Victory March."

Cool Rob Lee and His Rebel Rockers Shake the Civil War, which contains "Rocking Bonnie Blue Flag," "You Ain't Nothing but a Carpetbagger," and "Just Before the Battle, Mother, Mambo."

Other top-selling albums are *Urias Cowfever and His Smoky Mountain Rail Fence Rompers Pick Out Songs of the Southern Secession,* and *The South African Hippopotamus Jawbone Band Plays Songs of Dixie.*

From *Birth of a Nation* and *Gone with the Wind* to Saturday Westerns, the Confederates continue to win the battle of the movie screen. Southern armies are usually pictured as outnumbered but not outfought; Southern officers as having a dash of chivalry not present in their Yankee foes. If the South loses, in a movie, it loses because it was overwhelmed by a force some one hundred times larger. In Western movies, the South has always won out at the end by rescuing a smaller Northern force from a horde of Apache Indians.

Perhaps there will be a movie titled *Whatever Happened to Robbie Lee?* in which all of the clichés

The heroic women

and maudlin lines that have been uttered in Civil War movies will be assembled for one last big gasp.

AGED PLANTATION OWNER TO SON IN NO UNIFORM: "There's been a Tolliver in every war—so why are you standing there in your BVDs?"

AGED PLANTATION OWNER TO SWEET MAGNOLIA BLOSSOM, BOTH LOOKING FAR DOWN ROAD: "Don't worry, honey, he'll be back some day."

HEROIC SON TO MAGNOLIA BLOSSOM: "I'll be back some day and we'll build that little smokehouse for two."

MAGNOLIA BLOSSOM TO HERO: "I'll be waitin' by the stable door for your return."

of the South

GRIZZLED SERGEANT TO ELEGANTLY DRESSED MAJOR:
"It wuz us who did the fighting at Bull Run, Sharpsburg, etc., etc., and not you fancy officers."

ELEGANTLY DRESSED MAJOR TO GRIZZLED SERGEANT:
"You must think I like sending those men out there to be killed."

YOUNG HERO TO GRIZZLED SERGEANT: "Look, the Yankees are charging."

GRIZZLED SERGEANT: (*Calmly spitting tobacco juice*) "Save your powder, boy, they'll get a lot closer."

YOUNG HERO TO GRIZZLED SERGEANT: "Look—the Yankees are being ambushed by Apaches."

GRIZZLED SERGEANT TO ELEGANTLY DRESSED MAJOR:
"Hooray! We've saved the gold shipment that will buy foreign troops to help Robert E. Lee take Washington and win the War."

ELEGANTLY DRESSED MAJOR TO GRIZZLED SERGEANT:
"But they are Americans—we just can't let them be slaughtered by Indians."

(*Follows fifteen minutes of unnecessary drumbeating, incoherent shouts of "Mount up," bands playing medleys of Civil War songs.*)

ELEGANTLY DRESSED MAJOR: "Sergeant, move the men forward."

GRIZZLED SERGEANT: "Forward men."

YOUNG HERO TO FRIEND: "Look, we're moving forward."

(*Union and Confederate battleflags now stand side by side while soundtrack repeats medley of war songs till Indians are routed.*)

EMBARRASSED YOUNG UNION CAPTAIN FRESH FROM WEST POINT: "My compliments, sir."

ELEGANTLY DRESSED MAJOR TO EMBARRASSED YOUNG UNION CAPTAIN FRESH FROM WEST POINT: "My compliments too—let's cut this war jazz, split the gold, and invest in Western real estate."

EMBARRASSED YOUNG UNION CAPTAIN FRESH FROM WEST POINT TO ELEGANTLY DRESSED MAJOR: "Spoken like an American."

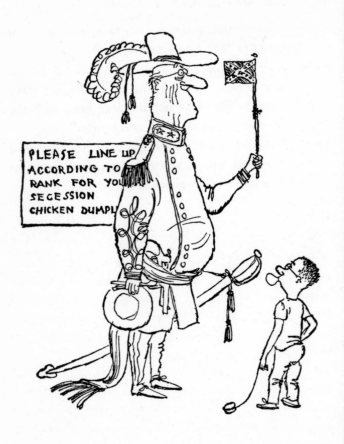

PLEASE LINE UP
ACCORDING TO
RANK FOR YOU[R]
SECESSION
CHICKEN DUMPL[INGS]

The Great Confederate Epidemic:
Centennialism, Roundtabilitis,
& Re-enactment Fever

Time was that if Podunk Corners wanted to commemorate the birthday of General Lockjaw Polk, nobody got very excited. The local cell unit of the Sobbing Sisters of the S.S. would head for the village statue and hang a wreath on its granite cartridge box; the ducktail-adorned local guard unit would fire a disinterested volley; and last year's 4-H Queen would read a grisly poem telling of General Polk's retreat.

Not so today. The local boys from the Chamber of Commerce, motel owners, cider and minié ball hucksters, and retired National Guard Colonels who never saw a live round of ammo, have joined forces to commemorate in style everything from the battle of

Gettysburg to the last mule in the Rebel army. Two groups have led the way in the present day race to commemorate—the centennial commission and the roundtable members.

The centennial commission, whether statewide or local, is usually comprised of the following members:

CHAIRMAN: An off-beat State College history teacher and Civil War buffoon whose last book sold two copies.

EXECUTIVE DIRECTOR: This post, which demands leg work and tail resting, is generally filled by an out-of-work and self-appointed "Colonel," who got his commission as a former auctioneer. He wears moth-chewed suede coats, splatters his droll conversation with references to "fathuh's division" and the "Yunkees," and displays on the wall behind his oversized desk a large map of Civil War campaigns, replete with numerous colored tacks.

THE COMMITTEE: No centennial commission would be complete without the Committee. The Committee is composed of influential state senators, battlefield motel owners, high brass of the Sobbing Sisters of the S.S., county judges, bored bank presidents who collect lead soldiers, and a solid phalanx of first class antiques such as family tree surgeons and museum operators. All of these people are affected with a strange and contagious malady known as "Centennialism." Basically, the disease Centennialism is the uncontrolled desire to commemorate.[1] The object of the centennial celebration makes no difference. If Robert E. Lee threw a corn cob at a pesky camp dog somewhere in the neighborhood, a commemoration ceremony will be held, complete with the planting of a gaudy, silvery-embossed highway marker. There is something magic about the figure 100, possibly the fact that it so closely resembles a one dollar mark.

The symptoms of Centennialism are easy to discern: the pulse quickens whenever the term "Confederate Monument" is mentioned; eyes dilate at the sight of an unmarked Civil War site; the nose twitches violently when within 500 yards of an unrestored Civil War breastworks; and extreme itching occurs, especially near the pocketbook, whenever the term "tourist" is mentioned. Naturally, the Centennial Committee plans all ceremonies within range of local motels and orange blossom honey stands operated by—surprise!—Committee members.

Centennialism is seen in two acute forms—"Roundtabilitis" and "Re-enactment Fever." The breeding place for many Civil War bugs is the Roundtable, made up of hapless individuals who have Roundtabilitis. A roundtable is not a roundtable at all, for the only table these Civil War buffs see is the game room bar. A typical Civil War roundtable might con-

[1] To make money.

sist of: a former shavetail second lieutenant who never tires of telling how he singlehandedly won the Battle of the Bulge; a frustrated plumber who always wanted to charge with Pickett; a henpecked electrician whose wife would not let him keep mummified generals in the house; and, almost always, a Confederate money dealer, who always "just happens to have" a slash mark III Leonidas Polk thirty-five dollar bill in his wallet for fellow members to fawn over.

Roundtables have more officers and ranks than the original Confederate army, which is saying quite a lot. Civil War buffoons do not stop with a president, secretary, and treasurer. *Everyone* is an officer. Such high offices are held as:

GUIDON BEARER: Takes down all the pin-ups after the meeting closes.

FORAGE MASTER: The leader of the advance on local tavern.

DRUM MAJOR: Hires the high stepper who entertains after the meeting is over.

COLOR GUARD: A delegation which writes angry letters whenever a Civil Rights Bill is before Congress.

Roundtables divide themselves into military units such as platoons, batteries, and squads of four for gin rummy. In almost every roundtable, one will find a member smitten with uniformitis (i.e., a mania for wearing the exact uniform and equipment that Gen-

eral Beauregard wore—right down to his ragged undershorts). This type of Civil War buffoon will accost you upon entering the meeting hall, and, with gleaming eyes, inform you that your forage cap should have a black worsted braid not over one-eighth of an inch wide. You hardly have time to run to the nearest surplus store to right the error when he jovially informs you that the chevron on your sleeve is not one inch above the position of the elbow joint. Feebly, you throw your regulation blue tunic around yourself to conceal more mistakes in dress, only to be informed that the single row of six brass buttons on your tunic does not extend to the waistline. Even when the buff attempts to maintain proper uniform standards, he can fall into error. One hapless Civil Warrior, whose roundtable wore shell jackets with eight brass buzzards on the gizzard, was arrested en route to the meeting for impersonating a highway patrol officer. Uniformitis is an expensive form of roundtabilitis. Surplus stores get rich on Civil War buffoons who troop in to purchase gray twill tunics, yellow silk sashes, gilt braid forage caps, and regulation cavalry boots fresh from the closeout of a motorcycle accessory supply house.

The minutes of a typical meeting:

7:00 P.M.—Bugle call to arms. Since Chief Bugler Leonidas Poke VII was too inebriated to blow, an

LP record of the South African Loyalist Corps Drill
Team was used.

7:10 P.M.—Pledge of allegiance to the Confederate
flag. During the pledge, the flagstand collapsed and
four states on the flag were soaked in the rum punch.

7:15 P.M.—The Grand Minutes Major removed his
cavalry hat and read the minutes of the last meeting.
Remarks concerning the argument over where to have
the annual parched corn and salt pork feed were
stricken from the records as too profane.

7:30 P.M.—The business meeting commenced.
Forty dollars was voted to send to the Wetumpka,
Tennessee, Ladies Trap Drum Regiment Auxiliary
to restore the statue of General Felix Zollicoffer,
whose right knee was crushed by a drunken bulldozer
operator.

7:45 P.M.—The Roundtable voted fifty dollars as
a cash award for the sixth grade student at Coontrot,
Kentucky, who writes the best essay on why the Confederacy would have won the War for Southern
Liberation if it had had more men.

8:00 P.M.—Discussion of possible new members.
Mr. Hobart Lumpkin was rejected by a 40 to 2 vote
because he has a cousin who lives in Michigan. Colonel Bluefield Allegheny, prominent stockraiser, was
unanimously accepted after promising to loan the
Roundtable his entire herd of fine Kentucky mules

for the re-enactment of the cavalry skirmish at Davis Ford, Tennessee.

8:30 P.M.—Grand Sergeant Major introduced the speaker for the evening, Lester B. Cockroach, Grand Imperial Cannon Swabber of the Maury County, Tennessee, Howitzer Drill Unit. Mr. Cockroach delivered a fine two hour lecture on "Where Nathan Bedford Forrest Crossed Duck River on November 29, 1864," complete with sound movie, colored slides, charts, and flannelgraphs.

10:30 P.M.—Recreation Hour was provided by Forage Master Tobe Jones. A fine performance was given by the Rebellettes, from Backwater, Mississippi. This fine precision exotic dancing team removed their regulation uniforms smartly to the tune of "Yellow Rose of Texas." Highlight of the evening's entertainment was an impressionistic dance representing the flags of the Confederacy.

12:00 Midnight—Following a lengthy Recreation Hour, club members, before departing for individual bivouacs, slaked their thirst at the Rebel canteen, a folding bar which fits smartly into the rear of the Civil War bookcase of host Herby Johnson.

Avid roundtables purchase elaborate outfits and organize drill teams to perform not only at local battle re-enactments and centennial celebrations, but at practically any event to which they are invited, whether the County Co-op Fertilizer Queen Pageant or a parade honoring the opening of a new agricultural extension service. The smaller the town, the more elaborate is the name and dress of the drill team. Hence, in Tennessee you might have the Ragweed County Flaming Zouave Dragoons composed of local feedstore employees riding plough mules.

Artillery units are also very popular. Local roundtables buy cannon from scrap iron jobbers or else "requisition them" from national military parks. The result might be the Watercress County, Kentucky, Royal Brass Napoleon Artillery Battery, consisting of one battered field piece too dangerous to fire. Casualties among these groups who insist upon demonstrating their inability to handle old weapons are larger than in most of the Civil War battles. Roundtables lose charter members by the caisson-load every time some cannon of ancient vintage is rammed up for a July 4 shoot-out. Avid roundtable members intent upon drill-team firing of decrepit rifles are frequently maimed when they put enough charge in a rabbit rifle to kill an elephant. At the centennial celebration of the birthday of General Cutlass Cotton-boll, held at Womply Springs, Mississippi, the fine artillery battery from Holly Bogs, Mississippi (which doubled as the volunteer fire department) put on a fine loading exhibition for the crowd gathered at the general's statue. However, one Bernie Zuck, assistant wheel greaser for the battery, dropped his rabbit-tobacco cigar into the firing pan of the cannon, and the fine statue of the general was reduced to a handsome sundial.

By far the most contagious form of Confederate sickness is Re-enactment Fever, which hits both round-table members and centennial commissions. One centennial organization has gone so far as to put out a book entitled, *Instructions for Organization, Equipment, and Uniform of Military Memorial Units,* which has more rules than the old Rebs had ever heard of. In previous years, when citizens wanted to join in a commemoration ceremony, they grabbed a ten-cent flag and marched with the band. Not so with those neo-Confederates smitten with Re-enactment Fever. The *minimum* of equipment demanded for participation in a Rebel wake includes uniforms, pistol, saber, cartridge box, canteen, saddle, blanket, bedroll, and preferably a horse—which explains why the Civil War is still a rich man's war and a poor man's fight.

Commissioners and roundtablers smitten with the fever will re-enact everything. The favorite re-enactment is the battle. Thousands of volunteers are available to portray Confederate soldiers; Union soldiers are drawn by lot because it has always been their lot to be the villain.

A typical Confederate army portrayed in a re-enactment of the battle of Indian Burp, Arkansas, might include:

COMMANDING GENERAL: General Hammus Hock, portrayed by State Senator and Chairman of the Historical Appropriations Committee I. O. Belch.

LIEUTENANT COMMANDER: Brigadier General Elijah Bullmoose, portrayed by I. O. Belch, Jr., son of Senator Belch, promising student and pool player at Grundy State College.

FIRST ARMY CORPS: The first corps, commanded by Colonel Ezra Spit (portrayed by prominent Burp County lawyer and prospective candidate for County Judge, Elias Hunk), is made up of boys from the Lacepants Military Academy Spotted Horse Troop.

SECOND CORPS: The second corps, commanded by Brigadier General William J. Hardeeup (portrayed by Humbert Plump, State Commander of the Sons of the Sobbing Sisters of the Southern Secession), are volunteers recruited from the State Highway Patrol.

CAVALRY: The cavalry battalion, commanded by Lieutenant General Nathan Bedford Furrier (portrayed by State Sobbing Sisters Vice Regent Miss Alma Plunk, who grew a handsome beard for the occasion), is composed of volunteers from Little Lord

Flauntitboy Riding Academy from Bourbonsnod, Kentucky.

ARTILLERY BATTERY: The artillery battery, commanded by Colonel Winchester Chainshot, is portrayed by the Nashville, Tennessee, Fifth Davidson County Light Mounted Napoleon Swabbers Battery, commanded by Guilford Snob, prominent Nashville wholesale plumbing parts salesman.

Special mention for the ceremonies should be given to:

Burp County Ladies' Aid Society, for help in removing the wounded when the artillery battery exploded.

Elijah Cob, Burp County Constable, for his help in directing traffic. Officer Cob wisely allowed only those automobiles bearing the sticker "Centennial Commission Official Car" to drive over the Federal breastworks in the final Confederate charge.

Sheriff Opie Jones, for his quick apprehension of fourteen Confederate infantrymen using live ammunition.

Mr. Lester Gooch, for his excellent operation of the sunglass concession located in the Confederate bivouac area. Mr. Gooch respectfully pulled the plugs out of the automatic vending machines during the reading of the "Ode to the South."

Warden Horace Jones of the Burp County Prison

Farm, who donated 300 trustees to portray the Federal army. And to the State Highway Patrol for recovering one corps of the Federal army, which fled the battlefield and the county in the heat of the day's battle.

Our Local Correspondent Reports
on the Re-enactment at
Goslin's Branch

It all started over the battle of Goslin's Branch. According to Miss Elsie Sloan at the county library, the fight was between Colonel Asthma M. C. F. Kilpatrick's 385th Arkansas Light Mounted Bragoon Horse Artillery and Brevet Lieutenant Colonel Wheezemeyer A. Hankin's Brigade of the 145th Rhode Island Mounted Fusileers (provisional). Most everybody around Goslin's Branch had forgot about the big battle till the Sobbing Sisters of the Southern Secession (Camp 452), commanded by Mrs. Tobe Potts (he's the fertilizer salesman over at Cave Springs), decided to build what they called in the county newspaper a "decent and fitting memorial to this decisive battle, the highwater mark of Confederate fortunes in the western part of Southeastern Tennessee."

Now I don't care much myself, 'cause everybody knows around here that the battle was fought over who was going to get the six hogs out of Junior Pott's grandfather's back pen down by Mingo Branch. Fact is, only real casualty was a Yankee forage master who ran into the outhouse while looking back over his shoulder. But this didn't make much difference. Camp 452 decided that some kind of stone ought to be put up to remember the event.

Well, that didn't exactly bother me either, except that they decided to put up a marker next to Augie Dodson's pond on the Sequatchie Road. Since they held the lease on the property, the Sobbing Sisters voted to fence the pond in, build a monument, and go down to the Tolliver Landing graveyard and haul up what's left of Colonel Winchester St. Lefant Potts.[1] Then they would bury the old bastard by the pond and only allow folks to fish there who could prove some way or other that their ancestors fought in the battle.[2]

That nailed the hide to the smokehouse. Everybody in this half of Sequatchie County knows that Augie Dodson's pond is the best bullhead hole west of the log dam on the Caney Fork River. For years it has been open to anybody who wanted to use it, so

[1] Tobe Pott's grandfather and Confederate commander in the battle.

[2] On the Confederate side.

long as he didn't let Si Mosby's sheep out of the south
field. Besides, this had always been the official meeting
place of the Cumberland Ridge Coon and Fox Hound
Breeders Association M.O.[3] Wasn't another place
west of Knoxville where a man could sit and drink
hard cider and fish bullets, and have a body's peace.

So I reckon I knew what to expect when the club
had its monthly meeting at the county line service
station the next night. By the time I got there, things
were going whole hog. I could see all twenty members
there, and most of them were already plastered on
Mrs. Sue Nell Mangum's homemade watermelon white
wine. Hubert Hill, Sunday School Superintendent
over at Cave Springs Two-Seed-in-the-Spirit-Re-
formed Evangelical and Running-Water-Baptism
Only Church was holding the floor—fact is, he was
lying on it (Hubert always could drink more than a
boar coon eating sorghum). "It's unconstitutional,
immoral, and a downright durn dirty trick," he
spluttered. "Why, everybody knows old Winchester
Potts was the biggest stud east of Elk River." Don't
think I'd argue that.

Fact is, the only fighting old Winchester did worth
anything was when the Yankees trapped him in bed
with some woman over at Horse Mill one December
night in 1862. Seems Colonel Potts, who had been
detached for "special service," fought his way clean
out of bed, past a whole squad of Yankee cavalry and

[3] Men only.

out the front door of the Stockfarmers' Hotel. Folks
said it was a right smart fight. Probably would have
been a sight more impressive if Winchester hadn't
caught his night shirt on the hitching post when he
jumped on his horse. According to all reports, Colonel
Potts had the honor of being the only naked cavalryman in Bragg's army that night in action on the
Shelbyville road.

Well, the club decided to send a committee to the
monthly meeting of the Sobbing Sisters to see what
we could do about keeping the pond open. Having
some Confederate ancestry myself (grandpa packed
cartridges at the Selma arsenal) I was chosen spokes-
man. When we got to the meeting room (basement of
the Baptist Church) the meeting had already started,
so we slipped in on the back row. Mrs. Tobe Potts,
the Imperial Sergeant-Major General, was reporting
on ways and means. She wasn't much to look at (had
a face like a gutted catfish) but she cut a right smart
figure in her uniform, even if her sword did keep
stabbing her big toe. Fact is, she was rumored to be
the only woman in town with a picture of Pickett's
charge on her left bicep.

After she reported, everybody stood up and sang
"Marching through New York." It was right catchy,
but Hobie Gilbert swore up and down that he'd heard
the tune before. Then Miss Sue Nelle Hawkins led the
pledge of allegiance to the South, at which time the
color guard from Miss Bessie Jones' Sunday School

class presented arms. Would have been right impressive if Miss Bessie hadn't swung her flag too soon and caught Sue Nelle across the ribs. Sue Nelle (boys at the pool hall claimed she had a pair of drawers made out of a battle flag) jumped like a goosed boar and told Miss Bessie to keep her durn hands off the regimental flags anyway.

Well, they got quieted down when the club sang their official Confederate hymn, "Never Grow Old," after which Mrs. Sam Sewell led a closing prayer for "continued peace and good will," which would have gone over better if she hadn't dropped a cartridge box right before she amened.

We saw we weren't doing any good, so we slipped out and went down to rest at the pool hall. Signs were already going up all over town about the big centennial celebration, and it looked like a real footstomper was in store, with bands, schoolteachers from State College reading all kinds of important papers, and all six candidates for sheriff on the program. The club held a meeting in the back room of the pool hall, but it was more like a funeral. Hobart Jones, had a face as long as a Plott hound when he reported there wasn't nothing in the deed at the courthouse that would keep 'em from planting old Colonel Potts at our bullhead hole. Besides, Augie Dodson's wife had done put the pressure on him to let the women use the pond. Seems she made him sleep on the couch for a week. At which he relented and not only let 'em use the pond, but got rooked into being appointed Lieutenant-Colonel of the Secession Auxiliary. Then Lick Sullivan, the official keeper of the club's foxhorn announced his retirement because of "circumstances beyond his control" (he weighed 120 and his wife 240). Seems the whole club just busted up, so we couldn't organize any opposition. Lem Wilkins joined the church and even gave up chewing, and Sam Washburn, the president, got thirty days for killing fox squirrels out of season.

The day of the big show arrived with only three of us left in the club. But one was driving a float and another hung one on at the pre-centennial fish fry, so that left just me. I hung around the pool hall until parade time. I guess I've seen five parades in my lifetime, but this was the biggest since a local girl won the Valley Sweet Potato Queen Contest back in '42.

In all I guess I counted three bands, including one fine eleven-piece one from the Monroe County Consolidated High School. This one has always been a big favorite of mine since drum majorette Lula Mae Shouse forgot to wear her tights in the 1950 "Bring Our Boys Back From Korea" Celebration. 'Course

I'm not even counting the drill team from the Ladies Temperance Society that carried signs saying to drink spring water and keep healthy. They clanked soft drink bottles in rhythm till they reached Doc Bufford's drugstore, where they fell out from exhaustion.

Then came the official party in the constable's car. It was an impressive group, even though the car threw a rod and they had to continue the parade in Opie Read's cattle truck. There was Major Gus Turner running for re-election, Miss Sue Nelle Hawkins, the Fertilizer Co-op Queen, and little Lancelot Pigg, the county spelling champion. Next I spotted Boy Scout Troop 599 from Oliver Springs, dressed in authentic Indian costumes. They looked right Indian, even if little Eddie Logan's headdress did have "Hoboken, New Jersey," painted on it.

I stepped in to march with the men's Sunday School class from Caney Fork, even though I didn't have my button that signified I'd read Second Chronicles twelve times. We were marching behind the county high school majorettes, who later complained that they kept getting pinched by a bunch of drunks. I can't hardly deny this, since when we made a hard right turn on the public square, the whole first row of the class, including the roll keeper, kept going straight into Bud's Tavern.

Well, the ceremonies at the pond began in a big way. Reverend Perkins opened with his talk on "The

Greater Confederate Moral Victory at Gettysburg," after which the local K.K.K. harmonica band played "All Quiet Along the Potomac Tonight." Then Miss Ophelia Cotton Gin, great-granddaughter of the famous Brevet Brigadier General Secession T. Cotton Gin, read the pledge of allegiance to the flag of the Fourth Tennessee Infantry. Then a constipated-looking teacher from State College started to read a right long paper on "Symbolism and Poetic Imagery in Confederate Field Battle Reports." I would have enjoyed it except Hobie Potts kept going to sleep beside me and slobbering on my battle flag.

Then came time for the burying ceremonies. The County Judge delivered a powerful oration on "Colonel Winchester Potts, Father, General, and Nation Builder." Right powerful speech—covered everything from the battle of Magna Charta clear through the causes of the Revolutionary War to the Battle of Primm's Smokehouse in 1864. When the Judge finished, he took a swig of Miss Willie Lumpkin's homemade gourd brandy, and nodded to the Boy Scout troop. A war surplus bugle blared out taps, and the burying was on.

The Sobbing Sisters had done it up, alright. To make it a more impressive sight, they'd decided to float the Colonel's coffin across the bullhead pond on what they called a funeral barge. 'Course it wasn't really nothing but two of Buck Collins' tractor inner-tubes and a bunch of nailed planks. But when the

bugle played Taps, they started paddling the raft across the pond. I could tell right off it was loaded a mite heavy. Besides Old Winchester and his coffin, there was an official honor guard (Tobe Wilkins and his rabbit gun), and a full delegation of the Sobbing Sisters aboard.

Right off, things went wrong. Just as they neared the bank, the hired mourners from Cave Springs Church burst into singing "He Arose," but Augie's prize sow, cooling off in the mud on the shallow bottom, woke up at the noise and raised up just as the funeral barge floated over. The raft flipped and threw the whole bunch into the bullhead hole—honor guard, Sobbing Sisters, and Colonel Potts still riding in his casket. Somebody jumped in and dragged the ladies out of the mud while others finally got a rope on the coffin, which was floating toward the mill dam. Then they hauled the Colonel ashore for the burying.

Reverend Perkins, by this time a little stout with the gourd wine, muttered a few verses, gazed into the sky, and whispered through his beard to the pallbearers to hurry up and get the bastard planted. And then it happened. The Colonel's waterlogged casket gave way at the bottom, and the mortal remains of the old boy rattled into the grave—all, that is, except a small medal which fell at the Judge's feet. "Dear friends," he spluttered, "Providence has allowed us a brief glimpse at a war trophy of this venerable patriot." He cleared his throat, accidentally spit in the grave, and read the inscription. "To Colonel Winchester Potts, for four years' service behind the Rebel lines as a spy. Best regards, Major General U. S. Grant, U.S.A."

Well, that was last month, and rumor has it that the Sobbing Sisters have disbanded and are now weaving potholders instead. I don't know why they took it so hard. I thought it was right enjoyable—so enjoyable that I reckon I'll mosey down to Chattanooga next month. I hear tell they're planning a big celebration there, too. Guess I'll go—that is, if the bullheads quit biting!

> Your correspondent,
> *Ezra Buttrey*

*Atlas of Dull, Inconsequential &
Unimportant Places Not to Visit
on a Centennial Tour of
Confederate Battlefields*

Northern tourists in the South have always needed
protection from crumbling Confederate statues of
Braxton Braggs, imitation dogwood, and hush pup-
pies with Mickies in them. Most guide books are out
of date because so many sites, especially graveyards,
have been moved to make room for TVA. Many an
old state's righter either turned over in his grave or
got turned out of it by this phase of the New Deal.

The following guide is provided for tourists who
plan to attend any of the 1,001 battle re-enactment
blow-outs that will ravage the South during the centennial celebration. The pace of the re-enactments is
proceeding so rapidly that many Southerners claim
they are already in a Second Reconstruction, which

is not much like a second honeymoon unless the Supreme Court looks like your mother-in-law.

This tour will proceed as follows: Lexington, Kentucky–Gunlock, Tennessee–Burp's Corner, Georgia —Lynchmob, Mississippi–New Orleans, Louisiana via U.S. 31, U.S. 41, U.S. Grant and General Sherman, State Route 10½, sixteen fox trails, and a creekbed. To confuse the tourist, the tour is described in a manner similar to the descriptions of tours in the American Guide Series.

Mileage

.666¼: Lexington, Kentucky. A quiet and charming town, Lexington is the birthplace of General Philander Crust, C.S.A., 1840–1865. General Crust, one of the 546 boy heroes of the Confederacy [which makes us think somebody's *kidding*], was killed at Cowpile, Alabama, in 1865, when his faithful horse Terence kicked six soldiers and one nearby cannon shell. General Crust, dying in the arms of his orderly Fitzgerald who was busy picking the general's pockets, uttered those famous words, "Ouch!" His home is now run by the Sobbing Sisters of the Southern Secession, Old Horse Chapter, and is operated by the old antiques as a museum.

41.1. At this point the road ascends Goose Mountain. At 42.3, right 6 miles to dry ford, cross and follow hog path 55 feet to Lonesome Rock. At Lonesome Rock, tradition says all Confederate generals

who ever admitted losing a battle wrote their names
—both of them.

51.6: Left, 6 miles, then east 5 miles on Peapatch
Turnpike to home of Luster Mintjulep, popular
Blowhard County Secession leader. Here one sees the
famous Mintjulep smokehouse, where other hams
were cured.

62.3: Highway crosses Tennessee line.

62.4: Speed Trap.

62.5: Office of Justice of the Peace.

62.6: Loan Office.

74.999: Right 6 miles to the curve overlooking the
Sowbelly Fork of the East Branch of North Shin-
bone Creek is the beautiful Marsha Falls, named for
a local Southern belle who loved to kick the gong
around. Local superstition says that underneath the
falls was a favorite hiding place for Yankee soldiers
—and Marsha.

85.4: Left 6 miles to Big Piggut Church National
Cemetery. Six Confederate soldiers who died from
overeating country ham were buried in June 1862.
The graves are marked and cared for by the S.S.S.S.,
Humbert Burp Chapter. Donations are appreciated.
Leave them with the kindly old sexton or if he is
absent, put them on the front seat of his sports con-
vertible.

90.2: The highway gently traverses Hog Ridge
and drops suddenly. After picking yourself up, continue across Turkey Ulcer Creek. From the bridge,

92.1, one sees the famous Losers Leap. Tradition has it that General A. S. S. St. Fluke, U.S.A., committed suicide here after surrendering his mountain garrison to a platoon of folksingers.

98.9: BLUE BOILING SPRINGS. Here on the Cumberland Mountain range is located a century-old spa and health resort. Chalybeate springs pour forth large quantities of mineral water. Blue Boiling Springs is a growing community, consisting of one hotel, one general store [with a *new* meat chopper], and forty-six Confederate monuments. At the world-famous

Crawl Inn Hotel, Miss Sue Nelle Goldenrod, called by some who lived to regret it the poet laureatess of the Confederacy, wrote 400 stanzas of her most famous poem, "The Death of General Zollicoffer at Mill Springs, Kentucky."

100.1: Right .2 mile to Tinkling Spring. (Caution! There is a narrow foot trail to the spring—use safety harness. Visitors should check with the First Aid station before descending.) Soldiers from both armies drank together at the spring, if they ran out of booze, they drank out of the spring. Whether they wore the blue or the gray, both sides wore hangovers.

128.6: Left .6 mile to a frog pond, right 8 miles to Robber's Cave. This cave was once the hideout of notorious Rebel outlaws and robbers led by the infamous Fleecem Jones. Today the cave is owned by another operator, Fleecem Jones III, who in dealing with tourists stopping at the cave, carries on in the great tradition of his ancestors. Right .2 mile to the Grand Hall of Glittering Columns and the Palisaded Fountain of Snowfall of Stalactite and the Stalagmite Grand Ballroom of Flowing Onyx. In this unpretentious room, cave formations (made of plaster by Fleecem Jones III in his workshop), hang from the wall. On the ceiling of the room can be seen the inscribed names of various Federal soldiers who hid out in the cave. The fact that the names appear to be written with a ball-point pen causes some slight doubt as to the authenticity of these inscriptions.

139.6: Herbie Peatmoss' Civil War Museum and Gift Shop. (Park in back lot next to lifesize model of Abraham Lincoln, insert a quarter and the mechanical Lincoln will split a rail. Insert a dollar and he will save the Union.) A side trip from Peatmoss' can be made on burros with cavalry saddles. Each tourist can thus ride his ass to the site of Fort Plumby, where for five dollars, he can witness the Civil War centennial re-enactment of the surrender of Fort Plumby, January 5, 1864, by Private Silas Gooch, Company B, Fifth Hogkill County, Tennessee Mounted Flaming Zouaves, to the Smoky Bear Brigade of U.S. Partisan Rangers. For an additional ten dollars, tourists can witness an endorsed national Civil War centennial re-enactment of the hanging of Private Gooch, sponsored by the Whoopee County, Alabama, Civil War Round Table. Donations are required for the memorial fund for those who volunteer to portray Private Gooch. For an additional ten dollars, the guide will get you back through the woods to Peatmoss' Gift Shop, where the tourists are hung.

While in the gift shop, visit the lovely museum sponsored by the General Simon Bolivar Bucket Chapter of the S.S.S.S. A large collection of old Confederates and old Confederate items can be found here. See especially little Sue Nell Peatmoss' collection of stuffed animals and Confederate brigadier-generals. Other interesting items include a stump on which General Robert E. Lee sat while being treated

by a surgeon for athlete's foot, and a rabbit's foot once owned by Stonewall Jackson's pet rabbit, John C. Fremont. Of special interest is the stuffed horse, Horace, favorite mount of Corporal Buford Plunk.

After visiting the museum, tourists are invited to purchase gifts in the tourist craft shop, where crafty salesmen are ready to sell genuine handicraft items made in the vicinity by local people. Among the locally-made items which can be bought here are: handmade Inca Indian Silver Hammered Zipper Flys, handmade Smoky Mountain Pottery, hand-made Ozark Mountain Pottery, handmade Rocky Mountain Pottery, handmade mountains. Other items include authentic Civil War bullets, used modern bullet moulds, and genuine Civil War uniforms and rifles [used only in old centennial celebrations].

141.2: Georgia State Line. Buy a peach and help the Klan.

156.2: The highway climbs to the top of the Smoky Mountain range [this is some feat in itself for there are few climbing highways]. Atop Bugaboo Gap is a large aluminum arrowhead, a memorial to the bri-gade of Cherokee Indians, led by Lt. Col. Sitting Bullregard, who defeated a detachment of Sherman's army marching through Georgia. The descendants continue on in the traditions of their sacred fathers by scalping every tourist who stops at the Gap. Two miles west is a foot trail and an outdoor amphitheatre, where nightly performances are given of the pageant,

"The Red in the Confederate Flag, Its Origin, History, and Meaning to Future Confederate Descendants." This six-hour play is sponsored by the Cracked Pottery Chapter of the S.S.S.S. All proceeds from the play go toward work on the 300-foot high face of General Leonidas Polk being carved on the face of the mountain.

171.4: The highway crosses Bumbling Branch. West .2 mile to the spot where Georgia Congressman Fatback Sowlasses announced his candidacy for re-election to the Confederate Congress in 1864. His speech was interrupted by the approach of Sherman's army and this brave and resourceful southern patriot immediately announced his candidacy for the United States Congress.

189.4: Little Pig's Eye Battlefield Museum and Chenille Bedspread Shop. This shop is operated by the ladies' auxiliary of the Sons of the Butternuts, an organization of Confederate ancestors. Confident of their cause, these Sons of the Butternuts, known as SOB's for short, operated a confidence game by selling Georgia chenille bedspreads made in Brooklyn, thus proving the adage, "If you can't outstich 'em, join 'em." The bedspreads may be bought in a variety of familiar patterns, including the famous "Birth of Stonewall Jackson's Horse," a diagram of Jefferson Davis' family tree, and a print showing the total number of Union casualties in the war. Proceeds from this blanket sale of bedspreads will go toward the centennial re-enactment of Lincoln's assassination, which is presented each week at the SOB's Bayonet Bread Bake and Parched Corn Supper sponsored by the Goosegrease Country Rifle Drill team. The museum may be reached by automobile; train service has been temporarily discontinued—for the past hundred years.

189.5: A large cast iron hog painted Confederate gray marks the site of the battle of Little Pig's Eye Creek. In 1864, the advance of Sherman's 80,000 troops was temporarily halted at the creek bridge by one Willard Slump, who operated the toll bridge over the creek. Placing himself squarely in the path of Sherman's army, this brave private citizen defied

General Sherman enjoying the hospitality of the South

General Sherman to march his troops across the bridge without paying a toll for each soldier. General Sherman replied, "In a Pig's Eye," and ordered the troops forward as Willard Slump held firm. The army advanced. His ancestors are invited to drop by on weekends and help look for Willard.

200.4: Alabama State Line. Watch for fallen stars in road.

200.9: Left 500 yards to an ancient trysting place for soldiers and their sweethearts, Crumbly's Well. This handsome glass brick and neon tubing structure was built by Enoch Crumbly, early Alabama pioneer and confidence man. Superstition has it that coins (especially large coins such as silver dollars) bring good luck when tossed into this antique structure. The good luck is usually brought to Enoch Crumbly, Jr., who cleans out the well after dark every night.

250.4¼: Grave of Old Wroxton. (See caretaker at Two-Seed-in-the Spirit Evangelical Church, Conservative Branch, for the key to the gate, or else just kick in the rusty iron fence.) Here under a magnificent stone sculpture of the Alabama Secession Convention is buried Old Wroxton, favorite mount of Senator Sidemeat, former grand regent, imperial viceroy and flag furler of the Sons of the Confederacy. Wroxton served his master well until 1924, when, as the Senator was out riding around his sassafras plantation, he accidentally jabbed an "Elect Calvin Coolidge" button in the horse's rump. The animal tossed his master into a convenient barbecue fire, giving birth to the name, "Southern fire eater."

300.2: Southernsnobobia. Right .1 mile on road lined with dead magnolia leaves to this palatial mansion. Built by Confederate statesman B. Weevil Moore, the house was designed by a traveling architect, who, when he passed on took Mrs. Moore who wanted more, with him. Colonel Moore lived in seclusion at the house for two weeks before he married again. His second wife, a distant relative of Grover Cleveland, is reported by local tradition to have had a very handsome moustache.

400½: Mississippi line. All trucks and buses must stop for inspection at the State Pest Control Station. Here the State attempts to halt entry of the boll weevil, cotton worm, and other things that are bugging Mississippi.

450: Muster Ground. Located under a clump of oaks, was the muster ground of the Tallapoopoochie County Artillery. This handsome company of 200 local dignitaries and six mules, a total of 206 jackasses, met weekly during the Civil War to drill and to petition their congressman for a cannon.

500.7: Forks of the Loolapoolooza River. Here, where the Watachiee Swamp is traversed by Tallachusetee Creek which runs into Wishahuskiee River which joins Sam's Pond, is the Forks of the Loolapoolooza River State Historical Monument. In 1864, Nathan Bedspring Forrest with fifteen Confederate troops and a fine battalion of Southern pool hall roustabouts, ambushed a regiment of Federal marshals guarding a wagon train of confiscated country hams. The Federal commander, commenting on the ambush, gave birth to the expression, "I couldn't see Forrest for the trees."

Re-enactment blues

Field piece

*Dictionary of Important
Civil War Terms to be Used
in Unimportant Conversations
by Insignificant People*

CASHIERED—One who was dismissed from the army was cashiered—thus he paid the price for his faults.

CHAINSHOTS—Chainshots were soldiers who were heavy drinkers.

DEPOTS—Depots were latrines used by German-speaking regiments.

DETACHED BASTION—This was a type of fortification. It was also a SOB on special assignment.

DRAGOONS—Dragoons were mounted infantry who were considered to be monsters by local citizens.

DRUMMER—A name applied to cowardly soldiers who beat it when a battle began.

ESCARP—A type of fortification. Also a French catfish.

FIELD PIECE—A camp follower.

FIELD TACTICS—Field tactics was the art of making hay with a farmer's daughter.

FIRE BALL—Fire balls were shells that flashed at night, or officers that flashed in daylight.

GRENADIERS—Female hand grenades.

GUIDES—Guides were friendly citizens who guided troops to enemy armies or friendly arms.

GUNNER'S PINCERS—These were devices used to set off a cannon, or a girl.

KNAPSACK—A soldier's bed.

LIGHT INFANTRY—Troops commanded by officers who carried no weight in Washington.

LOOPHOLES—Loopholes were holes that soldiers fired through and that generals who made mistakes crawled through.

LUNETTE—A type of trench dug by an insane officer.

MESS—Where and what Confederate soldiers ate.

MUSTER ROLLS—Stale Confederate bread.

PONTOON—A small-sized poltroon.

POWDER FLASK—A pocket flask loaded with gunpowder, which soldiers thought was a downright waste of space.

QUAKER GUNS—These were phony cannon made from logs and painted black to deceive the enemy, the Penn being mightier than the sword.

SEXTANT—Sextants were devices used by sailors for measuring distances around oceans and women.

SPLINTER PROOF—The splinter proof was a safety shelter for Federal soldiers during enemy attacks. During enemy attacks, Federal sailors hid in shrink proofs.

SPURS—Spurs were worn by cavalrymen and by chickens. To an infantryman, they were one and the same.

TELESCOPIC SIGHTS—Telescopic sights were used by sharpshooters, as well as by troops stationed near nurses' quarters.

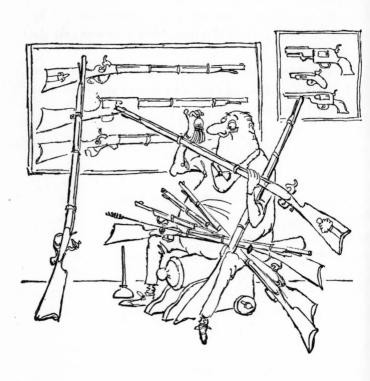

Confederama, Americana, Junkarama—
A Layman's Guide
to Civil War Relics

The present-day Confederama craze has turned many previously law-abiding citizens into first-class kleptomaniacs who chip away at old bricks, dig up military parks in the dead of the night, and bilk sweet old farm ladies out of grandpa's sword. Collecting Civil War "relics" has become a status symbol. The layman's collection *must* contain these items if it is to be considered worthy:

1. A Genuine Confederate Bayonet—Most Rebs were too poor to afford a rifle, much less a bayonet. If it were not for the Spanish-American war, there would be a severe shortage of Confederate bayonets.

2. A Genuine Confederate General's sword— Most of these are old Masonic swords to be had

at attractive prices in a Newark, New Jersey pawn shop.

3. A Civil War Canteen—Usually a surplus Boy Scout job picked up at an abandoned Tenderfoot campsite.

4. A Cannonball from Shiloh—Every collector has one. There are more old pieces of lead floating around labeled Shiloh cannonballs than there were cannonballs in the whole Confederate army.

5. A Cartridge Box—Spend five minutes in the den of a Civil War buffoon and he'll shove a crumbling mass of rust into your palm and brag about his CW cartridge box. Look close: it may be a rusty sardine can.

6. A Confederate Bullet—The buff will thrust upon you a battered mass of lead that resembles a fishing sinker chewed by a record walleyed pike.

Serious collectors spend hundreds of dollars each year prowling attics and roadside gyp parlors for everything from antique lithographs of Robert E. Lee's family to a button from General Cornsilk's truss. By far the most rabid collector is the one smitten with *metal detectoratis*. Given a war surplus, German mine detector and the scent of a minié ball, this jerk would plough through the Hanging Gardens of Babylon if he thought it would produce Jeb Stuart's shoe heel. Elaborate outfits include ear phones, metal detector, and automatic shovels which dig while a hidden recorder plays "Dixie." One can scarcely go to a party without some Civil War buff, foaming at the mouth, and dumping a half dozen grimy objects into your hands which although they look like tire weights, might with a lot of imagination, resemble minié balls.

Another collector to be avoided is the lead soldier addict. He will happily shell out five bucks for a lead Robert Lee giving a hand salute; ten dollars for R. E. L. looking through field glasses; and twenty-five dollars if he is thumbing his nose at the Yankees. Bootleg firms offer more interesting lead soldiers, such as female spies paying for information. The only bright spot in the future of a leadsman is that if he tires of his hobby he is way ahead on fishing tackle.

One sidesteps the metal detector fiend and the collector of lead soldiers only to cope with the egghead division of Confederatassa—the Confederate stamp collector. Confederate stamps were quite unimpressive, their texture resembling that of a tax stamp on a three-cent tobacco sack. Rebel envelopes were always adorned with maudlin scenes showing General Zollicoffer being mortally wounded at Mill Springs, Kentucky, or a sentimental poem to the girl in the cornhusk dress back in Haysack, Kentucky. Pity the poor cocktail party guest who gets cornered in a discussion over the virtues of handstamped pads over postmasters' provisions.

Should the layman be confronted with a collector

and find himself hard pressed to carry on an intelligent conversation, we include below a brief glossary of remarks for viewing Confederatassa collections.

"My, but that bayonet looks sharp to be so old." (don't comment on the rust-colored stain. It's rust.)

"Let's see, how was this musket fired, anyhow." (Stamps you as a lover of firearms.)

"A cannonball from Richmond? ... I have a cousin who lives in Lynchburg." (Shows you're well connected.)

"My great-grandfather had a whole trunk of this old Confederate money, but he burned it." (Congratulations—you have begun the Class-A category of shaggy dog story of the Civil War.)

"I have some old bullets in a shoe box at home you might be interested in." (Guarantees you a dinner invitation.)

Should the layman choose to collect, he will have no trouble in finding items to buy. Confederatassa is big business today. Someone is always willing to unload some old lead bullets, a rusty piece of a rifle, tin can fragments, or train conductor's buttons, and call them relics of Gettysburg. Running equally strong is the gadget trade. For several shekels anyone may purchase a Confederate lighter, cigarette case, socks, tie, belt buckle, pin, tee shirt, hat, teaspoons, salt and pepper shakers, cup and saucer, or even jockey shorts.

However, there are two pitfalls to avoid at all cost —the roadside museum and the catalog. The roadside museum is a combination of old junk under glass and new junk on a sales counter. Fifty miles before the traveler reaches the museum, he spies gaudy signs draping the roadside heralding "Genuine Museum, Gift Shop and Wild Animal Museum." After forty-nine more miles of cherry cider, chenille, and chocolate praline advertisements, the exhausted traveler stops at the museum to recover himself. Treading his way carefully over piles of rusty cannon balls and stuffed bears, he pays a "free will offering" to see the same kind of junk he has in his basement, and plunks down four bits for a Confederate teaspoon made in Tokyo.

More beguiling are the mail order house catalogs that push old and new Confederatassa. They pride themselves in terming their products Confederama, Americana, Railroadana.[1]

To help the reader avoid mistaking Arkansas hog guns for "genuine" Kentucky rifles and paying five dollars for a CSA belt buckle picked up at Bull Run via a Chicago moulding factory, a brief catalog to Confederatassa is included here.

GAMES

Civil War games are currently very popular. Board and dice games are available for all prominent battles such as Gettysburg, Chancellorsville, Pea Ridge, and Gauley Bridge. Plan your own battle

[1] "Ana" is a catchall for junk.

You find a knapsack full of Confederate money—go to Yazoo City and try to spend it.

WATERPROOF LA.

DOG WALK KY.

That was Gen. Lee you just backed your horse into—turn in your uniform.

...'S NECK VA.

BONEYARD TENN.
Go back to Hazel Bottom. Remember Hazel Bottom?

CHEESECAKE CHURCH VA.
A beautiful female enemy spy enters your tent—play it by ear.

MORNING SUN TENN.

SCROUNGEVILLE TENN.
Are you having a good time?

GRANT'S H.Q.: BAR CLOSES AT 11 O'CLOCK

MONO

A TOUR OF THE LESSER KN...
BATTLE AREAS OF THE C.W.

DON'T BOTHER TO LOOK IT UP—THESE ARE ACTUAL NAMES OF BATTLES, PAL.

GO ➤

A Minié ball has just gone through the top of your hat — yell like hell and go to the nearest field hospital.

BUZZARD ROOST GAP GA.
Put on your grandfather's forage cap and move up 1 square.

SHANGHAI MO.
Take it off—you look terrible.

SCATTERVILLE
Your canteen sprung a leak... to Waterproo...

DUCK RUN M...

You left your c...
back at Marrow...
—go and get t...

HAZEL BOTTOM MO.

Well here you are
at Hazel Bottom.

GOOSE CREEK VA.

You have just
sat down on
your bayonet—
congratulations!

FRYING PAN VA.

YAZOO CITY MISS.

You find a bee in
your coffee cup—
go back to Cowskin.

MOSQUITO INLET FLA.

Don't waste
precious time here
—push on to
Cheesecake Church.

...ONY

LEE'S H.Q.

WHITE TIE
PLEASE

SNICKER'S GAP VA.

You receive new
socks in the mail
—advance to
Frying Pan.

...WSKIN MO.

MOSCOW TENN.

You are behind the
sorghum curtain—
lose 3 turns.

MARROWBONE KY.

You
collect $200
bounty money
go to Grant's H.Q.
and have a
whisky
sour.

strategy. Each game comes complete with a mummified brigadier general and live black powder for special effects.

CIGARETTE LIGHTERS

Wind-up musical box lighters are popular. A handsome version features a sixty-piece military band playing fourteen verses of "The Conquered Banner" while miniature rockets fire salvos into your cigar. For ministers, the usually "Forget Hell" inscription is replaced by "Forget, fudge!"

CONFEDERATE JEWELRY

Confederate tie pins are popular if a person does not mind walking around all day with a picture of General Joe Johnston on his stomach. Key chains and watch fobs are adorned with sharp-edged Confederate battleflags which neatly rip out the lining of your pockets.

CIVIL WAR HATS

At almost any battlefield site, one can spot a regiment of tourists walking around in caps that look like surplus from the Boer War. No self-respecting, starving, freezing, bald-headed Rebel would have adorned his pate with one of these ornaments that has everything on it but the Jefferson Davis family tree.

Confederate uniforms varied;
some were dressier than others

The Bonnie Blue Flop—
Confederate Strategy
& Tactics

Despite rumors to the contrary, the Confederacy *did* have a strategy in the Civil War. Several schools of opinion offered advice to Jeff Davis—who welcomed it like castor oil. The Beauregard school suggested concentrating all available Rebs for one big push. The only trouble was that Beauregard's ideas always required a couple of million men that Davis did not have. The Braxton Bragg school—win and retire— was popular, but as time went on Bragg did less of the former and more of the latter. Old Joe Johnston led the Fabian School, named for the ancient commander famous for his retreats. Fabian tactics was only a fancy name for getting the hell out of there.

Was Jefferson Davis a great strategist? Some point to photographs of Davis' furrowed brow and thoughtful expression and say he must have been. Actually, Davis suffered from headaches.

1. *Defensive-Offensive*—This was the heart of Confederate strategy, which explains why the Confederacy did not live longer. Basically, the idea was to sit on the defensive and wait for a favorable moment to attack.

This offensive type of defensive strategy was tried at least seven times during the War with disastrous results. In 1862 the first Rebel offensive was in Texas, where a band of Confederraros under General Henry Sibley (who invented the Sibley tent and sat in it most of the War), hoped to win New Mexico and Carlsbad Caverns for the Confederacy. All went as planned until Sibley suffered an inglorious defeat at Glorietta Pass, after which the Indians took over, scalping stray Rebs and robbing them of their belt buckles for their grandsons to resell.

Then in April 1862 the South attacked the North at Pittsburg Landing, Tennessee. Since it was against roundtable rules for North and South to call a battle by the same name, the Yankees refused to fight at Pittsburg Landing. Instead they fought at Shiloh, "the place of peace," where the Confeds tossed in their magnolias and hightailed to Corinth, Mississippi.

Fortunes were low for Jeff Davis' strategy until the summer of 1862, when Lee and Bragg tried a two-pronged invasion, or more correct, a prong and a half invasion. Lee was still apologizing to Davis for the not-too-Sharpsburg performance when Bragg roared into Kentucky, bourbon-bound. After a magnificent job of losing the whereabouts of the enemy's army and half of his own, of burning his supply dump before evacuating the supplies, and of fighting half of the Union army with a corporal's guard at Perryville, Bragg retreated to Tennessee. He salvaged only his tranquilizer wagon.

In 1863 Jeff Davis tried again. Robert E. Lee took his troops on a long July Fourth weekend to Pennsylvania, where he shot his bolt in a nutty attempt to outflank the Main line. A year later Lee tried again, sending Jubal Early on a raid up the Shenandoah Valley. He got as far as Washington where he sickened at the sight of the Lincoln Memorial and turned back.

The final great defensive-offensive move was the 1864 Nashville campaign. The Confederate Army of Tennessee, which changed commanders more often than underwear, was now commanded by John Bell Hood, the "Lion of the Confederacy." In a brilliant stroke, Hood forgot to lay all of the track on his supply railroad. Then he trapped the entire Yankee army off base, only to let it march by his campfires without even throwing a charcoal briquet. Finally he besieged Nashville, the strongest fortress West of Gibraltar, with a paltry 17,000 troops. When he lost the battle, Hood sat in his tent and cried.

2. *Defend Richmond*—Jeff Davis, Lee, and other Richmond Rebs were infested with a curious blindness of the left eye—they never knew there was a Western Confederacy. This disease, "Tidewateritis,"

made the individual believe that there was no general save Lee and that Stonewall was his prophet. Let Donelson fall, let Vicksburgians dine on mule tail soup, let the Army of Tennessee be commanded by Bragg —whatever calamity befell the Western Confederacy went unheeded to sniffers of the Shenandoah breeze. Confederate officials wanted the capital at Richmond so they could keep an eye on front-line operations. Their wives wanted the capital at Richmond so they could keep an eye on behind-the-lines operations.

3. *All We Want is to be Left Alone*—This touching cry was voiced in 1860 by thousands of peace-loving Rebels who wanted only to use their bowie knives, bullwhips, rifles, cannon, bayonets, and gunboats to kill small game like Harriet Beecher Stowe.

4. *Diplomacy*—Confederates hoped to whitemail Europe into supporting the South. The Rebels believed that "Cotton was king," and that England would aid the South if her supply ran low. But England, which was now using Egyptian cotton, maintained a Sphinx-like silence, and the Confederacy's efforts to reduce John Bull came to naught. The sly diplomat John Slidell then parley-vooed with Napoleon III but here the South's hopes were Waterlooed too. France was too busy frying tamales with Maximilian in Mexico to give aid. The only ruler who recognized the South was the Duke of Saxe-Coburg-Gotha. Most Southerners did not even know where his kingdom was. This was all right, because he did not know where the Confederacy was, either. The

most famous diplomatic episode of the War was the Trent affair. A Confederate diplomat's liaison with a Mrs. Trent.

5. *Geography*—It was very hard to combine Confederate movements in the East and West because Confederate leaders did not like integration. Activities overlapped and jealous generals refused to cooperate and took up their marbles and went back home.

Rebel historians always point out that the flow of rivers through the South put the Confederates at a disadvantage. This river question has long been the crying towel of modern Confederates. Robert E. Lee had a knapsack full of good rivers running West to East across the front of his lines, but Rebs always moan about the lack of barriers to the enemy's approach on Lee's front. In the West, where the rivers ran North to South, Rebs were really up a creek.

6. *Logistics*—The disparity between the two forces has long been a favorite sop for Sobbing Sisters. Memorial Day speakers always wax long on the Rebel army's shortage of men, munitions, and money. The North had 22 million people; the South had 5½ million whites and 3½ million slaves. Official figures show that the North's corn production was twice that of the South. The North produced ten times as many manufactured articles as did the South. What the South did produce—mint leaves, grouse-feather fans and banjoes—were not too useful at the Bloody Angle.

7. To fit his hog-jowl strategy, Jeff Davis had to find a set of tactics—the science of what troops do not do when they get to the battlefield. Rocking chair strategists ponder lovingly the droll military terms that made up Rebel tactics. Any Confederate battle was a "mass offensive." "Surprise" was what the Yankees always did to the Rebs. "Economy of force" meant saving a rock or two to throw during the next battle. And "irregular warfare"—all of it, from Sumter to Appomattox.

The three great tactical weapons of the Confederate army were the bullet, trench, and bayonet. Firepower was increased in the War by the use of the rifled-musket which fired a minié ball. The minié ball was a grooved bullet invented by a French soldier, Claude Minié, who wanted a bullet which spun after being fired. For putting a little English on the bullet, Minié was executed for treason.

At least eighty-one different types of shoulder weapons—not counting women spies—were used by the Confederates. This disparity of weapons did not really produce an ammunition problem. All Confederate rifles fired *poorly*. But the increased use of rifles did not produce changes in the age-old tactics of *fire* and *shock*. Fire was what the Confederates would have done if their powder had not always been wet. Shock was what they felt when the Union army did not disappear after they fired.

The nomenclature and procedure for a Confederate attack is generally as follows:

Skirmish line—A line of thin soldiers, offering small targets, moving ahead of the regular force. Obtaining members for this unit was no problem in Rebel armies—everyone was underweight.

Battle line—The battle line advanced at intervals of 7 feet, 6 inches, barring a fractional wind change whereby the entire column wheeled left at 7 foot intervals in flank formation. In sight of the enemy the Confederate line howled and yipped.

On to Richmond & Other Euphemisms—
A Concise Account of the
North's Strategy

Lincoln had no military training but after he learned that ten thousand biographers planned to do volumes on Northern military strategy, he took less interest in posing for pennies, and more interest in the war. He gave war operations top drawer priority because his cabinet demanded it.

When war broke out, both sides were using smooth-bores—evidence of this being found in Congress as well as the army.

The often-used smoothbore rifle was loaded at the muzzle—which meant that the soldier carried the bullets in his mouth, thus originating the term "armed to the teeth."

Many books were written to improve military tactics, the Union using as its final authority, William

Hardee's imaginatively entitled *Tactics*. In the original work, Hardee discussed at length such military concepts as right dress (tux and tails), attacks by columns (with special attention to Drew Pearson), formations (T and single wing, with an excessive number of generals wanting to play quarterback).

Most theories and plans for whipping the South have been devised in recent years by armchair strategists off their rockers. There are so many that an index is needed:

The DEFEND-WASHINGTON SCHOOL. Many Northerners feared the invasion of Washington by a large army of foreigners from the South, trying to take the relics from the National Museum. But Jeff Davis said no, insisting that the South had enough old relics walking around without importing any more. One attack was made, however, in 1862. A brigade of Southern genealogists stormed the garden of the Library of Congress and tried to steal a fine grove of family trees. The pedigree tracers intended to prune off the limbs of any of their trees which might have northern leanings. Protected by coats of arms, this daring, hand-picked group cut their way through a gallant regiment of the Massachusetts "We Met the Mayflower Club," and other allied families, to a notable victory.

The LINCOLN-WAS-HIS-OWN-GENERAL SCHOOL. Many people think that Lincoln was the greatest military strategist of the war. Even General Grant leaned on him after he'd had a few.

The U. S. GRANT SCHOOL. The latest fashion in American history is to "reconsider." Everyone is reconsidering Grant, and he now emerges as the world's most reconsidered general. At West Point, Grant's roommate was Jefferson Davis, but the two boys could not get along and were separated. Grant always regretted that they divided since Davis had the only portable distillery in the dormitory. In 1861 Grant was determined that Davis would not leave again.

U. S. Grant under a cloud

Just Before the Decisive Battle,
Mother

A discussion of what was the Civil War's most decisive battle can produce an argument almost as harsh as the subject: Was General Lee really an octaroon? According to government publications, there were 10,455 engagements fought between North and South. But just how many men does it take to have an engagement? Of the total number, only seventy-six were classified as "battles," while 6,377 were labeled "skirmishes." The Confederates had more descriptive terms for fights than they had money in the bank. Just whether or not a fight was a battle or a skirmish usually depended upon who got beat. Before reading a battle account, one should familiarize himself with the meaning of the following terms.

Campaign—What a General calls a maneuver if it is
   successful.

Reconnaissance—An unsuccessful maneuver.

Battle—A fight that the General wins.

Skirmish—A fight that a General loses.

Strategic Withdrawal—A fight in which a General
   gets the stuffing beat out of him.

Raid—A successful attack on a Union chickenhouse.

Scout—The farmer had buckshot.

Affair—What officers had with lady spies.

Capture—What Confederates did when they took
   possession of a farmhouse.

Occupation—What Confederates did if the farmer
   had a daughter.

Combat—What most generals never saw.
Siege—The successful capture of a distillery.
Operations—Poker games in the mess tent.
Expedition—A night sortie to a battlefield comfort
  station.

Even worse are the names of battles. An atlas of
Confederate operations is a lexicographer's night-
mare. The battle of Mill Springs, Kentucky is also
the battle of Logan's Crossroads, Fishing Creek, and
Somerset. Do not confuse the battle of Hog Mountain, Alabama, with that of Hog Jowl Valley, Alabama—the distinction is that the latter is also known
as Ladd's Valley. There were three battles at Paint
Rock Bridge, Alabama, eight battles at Fort Morgan,
and six battles at Mossy Creek, Tennessee. Also, Confederate states named battlefields in different ways.
Louisiana is swamped with battle names such as
Bayou Teche and Snaggy Point. Georgia goes back
to the Indians for names like Allatoona and Coosa-
ville Road. Maryland takes to the hills to name its
battles, such as the epic struggles of South Mountain and Crampton's Pass. Mississippi bogged down
in river bottom nomenclature. Dozens of battles are
named Tallahatchie River, Hatchie River, Wau-
hatchie River, or Birdhatchie River. The prize for
the zaniest battle names must be awarded jointly to
Kentucky and Tennessee. The Bluegrass state saw
encounters such as Dog Walk and Goose Creek Salt

Works. Tennessee was the scene of such great battles as Bobo's Crossroads and Rising Sun. And do not forget, something important must have happened at the battle of Elrod's Tan Yard in Alabama.

Another characteristic of Confederate battles was how they whizzed, roared, or sputtered. Impecunious light colonels, looking for a brigadier's bars, colored battle reports with fancy adjectives and purple prose that made a battlefield sound like a convention of the Association of Onomatopoeia Poets. Battlefield reports are cluttered with bloodthirsty expressions such as:

Roared	Kicked	Nudged	Fled
Whizzed	Knocked	Exploded	Ran
Sputtered	Drove	Shattered	Panicked
Popped	Stabbed	Soared	Routed
Crackled	Stung	Shrieked	Demoralized
Boomed	Jabbed	Shone	Retreated
Banged	Blew	Sparkled	Charged
Beat	Blared	Glittered	Drove
Broke	Trumpeted	Waved	Edged
Cracked	Gouged	Resounded	Slew
Mashed	Smashed	Recoiled	Killed
Pushed	Smacked	Scattered	Wounded
Shoved	Slammed	Cut	Maimed

Moreover, geographical landmarks were not just hills, creeks, and fields. Every Civil War battlefield has the same colorful set of landmarks:

Sunken Road	Mill
Peach Orchard	Abandoned Mill
Wheat Field	Somebody's Springs
Corn Field	Somebody's Ford
Stone Bridge	Mill Dam
Bloody Angle	Burnt Tavern
Plank Road	Burnt Farmhouse
Turnpike	Sulphur Springs
Stone Wall	Cedar Hill
Rail Fence	Cedar Knob
Locust Thicket	Cedar Mountain
Locust Grove	Cedar Springs
Hornet's Nest	Abandoned Railroad
Devil's Den	Red Barn
Rock Church	White Barn
Stone Church	Burnt Barn
Log Church	Raccoon Springs
Burnt Church	Somebody's Crossroads
Brick Church	Widow Somebody's House
Abandoned Church	Pine Knoll
Telegraph Road	Beech Grove

A congressional observer

10

I Wish I Could'a Gotten to the Land of Cotton— Bull Run to Petersburg

The Confederates moved their capital from Montgomery to Richmond because Davis preferred shells falling on Richmond to stars falling on Alabama. Richmond was a very important town, being the chief repository of genealogical records of Southern families. Simultaneously, General Joseph Johnston, and a Southern army composed of ten thousand brigadier generals marched toward Washington.

The two armies collided at an appropriately named creek—Bull Run, the scene of the first major engagement of the C.W. For every soldier on the field, there were always a dozen or so observers—Congressmen, artists, photographers, and book publishers ready with memoir contracts in hand.

At the loss of Bull Run, panic gripped Washington. Egg rolls on the White House lawn were canceled and the bar at the National Press Club was emptied. Work was suspended on the Lincoln Memorial, and the Pentagon was camouflaged as a square.

The Yankees appointed George McClellan as the new commander. He was called Little Napoleon by his troops because of his habit of tucking his arm inside his coat like the little emperor. Actually McClellan broke out into a rash every time he came within ten miles of battle. McClellan reorganized the army— the cavalry were assigned to combat duty instead of spending all their time giving pony rides to Lincoln's kids.

Meanwhile, Lincoln became impatient lest the war would not be over in time for him to enjoy the Washington theater season. In the summer of 1862 he told McClellan to march on Richmond via Williamsburg. McClellan protested that his army would get jammed up in the Williamsburg tourist traffic but Lincoln overruled him.

Lee scored once more at the Second Battle of Bull Run. The new Federal general was John Pope. Pope did not aim for Richmond, but instead headed for Cedar Mountain, Virginia, for reasons known only to himself and he's dead. At this engagement, General Phil Kearney was shot in the rearguard by a Rebel

(1) *It's not that we don't appreciate you, McClellan, but . . .*

(2) *We just thought you would be happier somewhere else, Pope . . .*

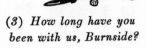

(3) *How long have you been with us, Burnside?*

(4) *Hooker, it's been nice knowing you....*

(5) *Well, Meade, I don't quite know how to say this, but ...*

(6) *Now that that's settled, Grant, how about one more short one?*

sharpshooter. This notable event has been understandably overlooked by local commemorating committees erecting statues.

Robert E. Lee began his offensive by invading Maryland but luckily for the North, a Union soldier found Lee's secret plans wrapped around a cigar. This was embarrassing for the South since, like all good Southern generals, Lee did not smoke, drink, chew, cuss, or wear union suits.

During the summer of 1863 things were dull while everyone waited for Vicksburg to surrender. To pick up the tempo, Jeff Davis and Lincoln flipped a penny [1] and decided to fight the decisive battle of the war at Gettysburg, Pennsylvania. Gettysburg was selected because of adequate hotel facilities for visiting British generals who would walk around after the battle and poke the ground with their swagger sticks.

In the interim, the Confederates moved against Gettysburg Woman's College, known on military maps as the Peach Orchard; the pickings were not so good and Confederate advances were repulsed.

With Generals Meade and Lee in charge, the teams met in the center of the field. The Federals won the toss and elected to receive. Lee had his choice of site and decided to defend the western end of the field so his good profile would be in front of Brady's cameras. The actual battle plan of the siege at Gettysburg (discovered in 1924 in the papers of Lee's aide-de-

[1] An Indian-head: Davis considered Lincoln pennies two-faced.

Mathew Brady covers the battlefront

You don't have to smile, General Sherman.

I wonder if you would mind holding up the battle for a few minutes, General Burnside?

Well, it's been nice meeting you at last, General Lee.

No thanks, I'll have my lunch in here; it's going to be a long exposure.

Say cheese.

It might make it easier, General, if you would try to visualize a little bird about here.

Could you hold the glass
in the other hand,
General Grant?

I'm awfully sorry, General
Pickett, but I seem to have
had my lens cover on—could
we have a retake?

No, I don't mind the bombardment, General,
but there seems to be a bee in here

camp and Traveler bather, Lieutenant Orphesu Swin-
burne Crust) called for Lee and Meade to clash atop
Cemetery Ridge. Orations were to be given on this
"high water mark" of the Confederacy and photographers were to take pictures. Old Rebels still maintain
that they were double-crossed as the Yankees actually
opened fire before the regimental bands had played
the first forty stanzas of Bonnie Blue Flag. But the
deceitful General Meade had suddenly remembered
that the next day was July Fourth, and being a Federal employee he was entitled to a long weekend provided his work was finished.

Uninformed of this treachery, the Confederates,
with uniforms pressed and sideburns combed, advanced across the Emmitsburg Road. Alas, the Union
guns opened and—so much for Gettysburg. There
are whole books on the subject of this three-day battle
for those who want to be bored senseless.[2]

But what of the action in the West? Operations in
the Mississippi River bogged down when Rebel engi-
neers built Fort Henry too close to the river and
water slopped over into their sputtering batteries.
After the capture of forts Henry and Donelson, the
Rebel fortress of Nashville fell to the enemy, despite a
heroic defense by the members of the Grand Ole
Opry. General Albert Sidney Johnston, who made his
last stand in Mississippi, was called the "Western

---

[2] Yes, this is the first book on the Civil War not to mention
Pickett's charge.

Lee" but was not successful because his horse was named Clyde and not Traveler. Successful Rebel Generals have always had horses with romantic names— Traveler, Thunderbolt, Old Sorrel, etc., but never Clyde. When Johnston hit Grant's army at Shiloh, Grant was out fishing. The Federal lines held and Grant was proclaimed a hero despite the fact that some Unionists complained that he had been drinking during the battle. This is a charge difficult to understand. *Of course* he was drinking. But he was drinking and *fishing*, not drinking and fighting. You can't expect a man to sit by a muddy Southern river waiting for the catfish to bite, without a jug.

Variations on the beard, mustache and hair-do—their integrations and sub-families.

Burnside (standard)

Curry Comb Burnside

Jungle

Imperial (classic)

Imperial (degenerale)

Chickamauga special

The Fauntleroy

TALIAFERRO TONSORIAL PARLOR

SHAVE AND HAIRCUT

25
15
10

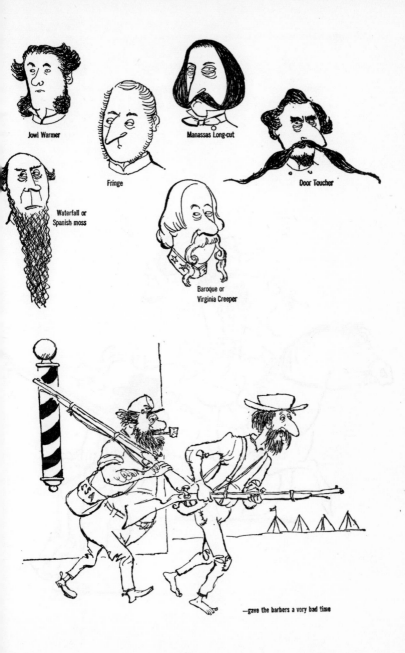

Jowl Warmer

Fringe

Manassas Long-cut

Door Toucher

Waterfall or
Spanish moss

Baroque or
Virginia Creeper

—gave the barbers a very bad time

Rebel Crass—
The Confederate Command System

ROBERT E. LEE—The inventor of knighthood, Lee finished his education at West Point second in his class. Against slavery and secession, he was also against coercion of the South and damnyankee interference. Standing foursquare on all major issues, Lee was offered a job in the Confederate army posing for postage stamps. A famous scene shows Lee making a decision while pacing the rose garden of Arlington all night. Actually, he was not thinking about the war but was worried about cutworms in his snapdragons.

NATHAN BEDFORD FORREST—Like all great men, Forrest was born in a log cabin, but by 1860 was worth over a million dollars, striking it rich as a slavetrader. He is known for his many famous sayings, among them:

"War means fighting and fighting means killing—so I quit."

"I got there fust with the mostus and left lastus with the leastus."

JOHN HUNT MORGAN—Morgan was famous for his raids into Kentucky to "liberate" people. These raids were touching examples of sacrifice, Kentuckians being so anxious for liberation that they hid behind trees and shot at Morgan to get his attention.

Battlers, Losers & Whitewash Jobs

Civil War buffs have long since passed the stage of hanging pictures of Lincoln and Grant in their den and calling it quits. Now, even the living-room walls are plastered with glossy eight-by-elevens of such illustrious figures as M. C. Zook, Israel B. Richardson, Benjamin Franklin Butler, and Daniel Sickles. Sickles, once Ambassador to Spain, was famous for shooting the son of Francis Scott Key, who had been seeing Sickle's wife by the dawn's early light.

George Armstrong Custer is remembered today by the many paintings of his last stand which hang on the walls of local taverns. This exploit is somewhat suspect, for Custer is shown standing with an arrow in his heart and is quoted as saying that the beer is mellow and light.

Benjamin F. Cheatham, Rebel general, had the amazing ability to cuss for forty-seven minutes without repeating a single word. Though he did not write his memoirs, it was said of Cheatham that his tongue was mightier than his sword.

Sinking the Mint Julep Navy

Lincoln proclaimed all Confederate sailors pirates. The U.S., however, had not signed the 1856 Paris Declaration making piracy illegal because we still thought there might be an honest buck in it somewhere.

Lincoln wanted Southern ports blockaded so the South could not receive its essential cargo—magnolia plants, foot-long cigars, and bullwhips.

Confederate Secretary of the Navy, Stephen Mallory, built ironclads—wooden boats with metal underwear—to break the blockade. The primitive Confederate submarine, the *H. L. Hunley*, established an early record for staying underwater—it's still there.

David Farragut, the naval hero of the Union, uttered his famous and generally misunderstood

An Ironclad on the Mississippi

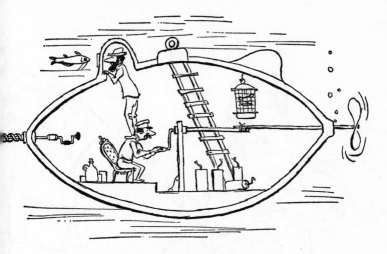

Primitive Confederate Submarine

words during the battle of Mobile Bay. Steaming into the bay, he saw that it was heavily mined and yelled to his skipper, "Damn it, look out for the torpedoes, full speed and head out of here."

Rebel gunboats were old steamboats armed with cotton bales and calliopes, much more valuable to Mark Twain and Stephen Foster in their line of work than to the Confederate admirals.

Abner Doubleday, "Father of baseball,"
orders his troops onto the field.

We're Tenting Tonight
on the Old Launching Pad—
The First of the Modern Wars

Ever since Cain did Abel in with a hunk of limestone, everyone has squabbled over which was the first of the so-called modern wars. Every war, from the battles of Alexander the Great to a Zulu tribal uprising has been scanned by experts looking for a first. Thus the 3rd Afghan war of 901 B.C. might be the first of the modern wars because, as any schoolboy knows, repeating slingshots were used for the first time. Since balloons, rockets, and railroads were of major importance during the Civil War, the experts have pinned this "modern" label on our War Between the States.

The subject of Civil War weapons is so complex that the ordinary buff needs to be thoroughly briefed before he clashes swords at roundtable meetings.

There, such questions as whether or not Corporal
Cleitus Foot was killed with a slash 2, mark 00, type
180 grain bullet assume major importance. One
subtle weapon was the prefabricated magnolia leaf,
used for psychological warfare. This imitation plant
emitted a strong odor which represented the smell of
the South on a dewy morning. A combination of a
damp museum, wormy Georgia canteloupe, the floor

The smell of the South on a dewy morning

of a smokehouse, and the breath of a foxhound—this scent combined with the melodies of Stephen Foster caused many a Union soldier to desert.

The demands of the tourist trade were, predictably, so great that efforts were made from the beginning to conserve the supply of minié balls. Also, the sharp-tipped umbrellas of the Virginia Old Dames, considered in retrospect to be the Confederacy's second most effective weapon.

Great improvements were made during the War in rockets and signals, especially by General Sherman who lit a Georgia mansion every night to tell his wife he would be home for Yom Kippur. Rocketry became so advanced that the Yankees published a brief digest of terms including:

BOOSTER—A good thing to drink before a battle.

BLAST OFF—What generals did at privates.

RE-ENTRY—Slipping back into camp AWOL.

Since hot air was plentiful, the balloon corps made great strides during the war. The most illustrious balloon was the *U. S. Grant*, which flew higher than a kite. Professor T. S. C. Lowe, the famous Union balloonist, was never shot down, because the Confederates always shot at random, which is why they missed Lowe.

Firearms underwent explosive developments. Dumdum bullets named for the Union generals were in constant use. Horse pistols had to be discarded due to difficulties the horses had in pulling the trigger.

Railroads were important for use in moving troops, visiting congressmen, and camp following. The Chesapeake and Ohio Railroad became a favorite target of the Confederates and was soon known as the Collapsed and Outoforder Railroad.

15

John Brown's Buddy—
The Confederate Medical Corps

For Johnny Reb, a fate worse than death was to be sent to a Confederate hospital. Anyone from a horse doctor to a medicine-show quack could get a surgeon's rank if they had the nerve and the equipment to hack off a limb. Books were provided by the Confederacy to guide the "doctors," including that notorious work, *A Manual of Military Surgery for the Use of Surgeons in the Confederate Army*. This book contained such chapters as "Amputations," "How to take Temperature," "Amputations," "The Art of Boiling Water," and "Amputations."

When the War started, the agricultural South was making hay instead of tourniquets and moonshine instead of castor oil. After Sumter, various attempts were made to get supplies. Blockade running was popular but not all blockade runners were as lucky as Rhett Butler. A medicine-smuggling trade was developed in Mexico but the unreliable Latin saw to it that the South received generous supplies of frozen chili and imitation Aztec jewelry. The government in order to combat the lack of medical supplies published *Resources of Southern Fields and Forests*, a manual which prescribed home remedies made from herbs. Two examples are:

For *Nausea or upset stomach*: Boil the roots of an Apple tree along with Peach tree leaves and drink the lukewarm mixture. This did not exactly cure the cause of the nausea but at least it brought the problem to the surface.

Swellings: Apply a poultice of onion and garlic. Some historians attribute the failure of the Confederate surprise attack at Shiloh to this offensive cure.

Many a sedate magnolia dowager's Georgia plantation was turned into a field hospital where some of the most heartrending scenes of the Confederacy were staged. Confederate memoirs are filled with memorable accounts of those patriotic women who tore their petticoats to shreds for bandages amid cries of "More, more" from the doctors and "Take it off" from the patients.

Whores d' Combat—Camp Life
in the Confederacy

A favorite form of entertainment was pillaging, or, as defined by the Sobbing Sisters, "requisitioning war materials." [1] Pillagers in the Confederate ranks were known by the genteel designation of "Partisans."

Farm animals of a dangerous nature, such as cows, chickens, ducks, and eggs, were often shot in self-defense by conscientious Rebs attempting to protect their comrades. Any Partisan knew that a goose always charges when wounded.

Alas, the Confederate knight was not immune to the temptations of the gentler sex. To listen to modern-day Sobbing Sisters, one would get the impression that all Rebs sat around the campfire at

[1] Anything you can get your hands on.

night singing "Home Sweet Home," knitting socks,
and roasting Yankees. But sex was a problem in the
Confederate army, as it had been in armies since the
days of the Trojan whorse. There were many petti-
coat brigades tenting on the old camp ground, these
"shock troops" providing the inspiration for such
rousing war songs as "All Quiet Along the Potomac
Tonight" and "Rose of Alabama." [2] The more enter-
prising camp followers smuggled maps and cannon
balls through the lines in their petticoats, thus reap-
ing income from two professions.[3] "Walks" around
the camp were quite popular, Rebels escorted the
"ladies" to inspect the fortifications by moonlight.

[2] Or "She ain't in the choir back home."
[3] Some great American fortunes were started in this way.

Because the South had always been a hospitable section, social disease became a problem. The situation was a pressing one, as evidenced by the large number of ballads of the era which were dedicated to the ladies willing to secede—or concede.

The real commander-in-chief

17

A Chapter on Abraham Lincoln Because Every Book on the Civil War Has a Chapter on Abraham Lincoln

Lincoln invented the log cabin. As a child he constantly borrowed books, forgetting to return them. This was the origin of the Lincoln library.

During the War, Lincoln came under editorial criticism which went so far as to question his fabled honesty. His detractors claimed that when he walked two miles to return two pennies to that poor widow, she protested, not out of sympathy but because actually he owed her fifty cents.

Lincoln's cabinet did not like him or his jokes. He often tried to read excerpts from Mark Twain and hilarious editorials from the *New York Times* to these gentlemen but they just did not dig him. As is so often the case, they didn't know he was a Great Man until after he was dead.

The radicals in Lincoln's administration were troublesome. While most Northerners wished to see Jeff Davis hang, the radicals wanted to tickle his feet as he swung. Thaddeus Stevens was the most famous of this group. The respect accorded to Stevens was so great that his fellow senators never used his pool cue in the Senate Conference Room.

*The venerable
Mr. Stevens*

Gastronomical Warfare—
Confederate Cooking

The Confederates never really had to win the War. All they had to do was to let the Yankees take over all of the territory they wanted and then feed them to death on a variety of dishes usually arranged under the misnomer, "Southern Cooking." One must try a few old recipes to get the real flavor of the Old South.

Mint Julep—No one who has ever set foot in Kentucky would think of leaving the State without plunking over a fistful of money for one scant shot of Old Tennis Shoes decorated with a cluster of greens served in a dimestore glass adorned with Confederate flags. Actually the same effect can be had by swilling vodka while chewing spearmint gum.

Grandmother Chess Pie—According to every Southerner, his grandmother was the best cook in the whole Confederacy. Every member of the Sobbing Sisters has an album full of old family "secret" recipes with "Chess pie" being a favorite among Southern family tree pruners. A sticky and loathsome concoction of eggs, butter, and too much sugar, chess pie is a Southern delight. If grandmother did the cooking, small wonder Rebel armies nigh starved to death.

Truckstop Pie—A greasy-spoon treat in Dixie is a gooey mess, called Southern Apple Pie, General Lee's Apple Pie, or Shenandoah Valley Apple Pie. Southerners always try to name their dishes after famous generals. Hence one has such delicacies as General Beauregard Creole Sauce and Braxton Bragg Sour Cream Dressing.

No Southern library is complete without a poorly bound volume of recipes scraped together by the Ladies Auxiliary. The fad has carried over into roadside eating places. Pecan pie becomes Georgia Confederate Pecan Pie Delight. Cold, hard rolls with enough yeast to kill a mule become Southern Plantation Bread. And a slab of ham that would be rejected in a breadline bears the name Virginia Old South Hickory Smoked Salt Cured Pecan Fed Hog Southern Ham. Words never fail the Southern cook, though recipes sometimes do.

Why Appomattox?

Grant's terms were generous: Confederate officers were allowed to keep their sidearms for the spring dueling season—or as they phrased it, "spring planting." Several of the Dixie states were permitted valuable concessions for the forthcoming Centennial celebration. Virginia received the apple cider monopoly, Kentucky the stringed tie and frozen chicken pot pie concession, Tennessee the Smoky Mountain handwoven BVD distributorship, Georgia the chenille-spread franchise, and Mississippi received a monopoly on bedsheets.

Before posing for the signing of the surrender, Lee and Grant carefully adjusted their public images.

Lee was to bear the image of an eagle with a broken wing, and Grant that of an Old Crow.

Lee went into semiretirement, buying a half-interest in Washington and Lee University. He spent the remainder of his life growing handsomer and handsomer and teaching classes in military strategy. Grant went into politics briefly and made a mess of it.

In order to qualify as a professional Confederate, answer three out of five of the following, grade yourself, and pick up your diploma at any convenient way station along U.S. 41:

1. General Lee once called General Grant a —— —— —— ——. (Use imagination on this one.)

2. Longstreet was late arriving at Gettysburg because —— ——. (Who can say you're wrong? Even Bruce Catton wasn't there.)

3. Traveler's favorite food was ——.

4. John Bell Hood's worst defeat was at ——. (Wide range of choices.)

5. Stonewall Jackson's favorite color was ——.

Get Right with the Confederacy, Brother— The War Nobody Lost

The last shots were fired at Appomattox and Benton-ville, when Lee and Joe Johnston tossed in the cartridge box. Think so? Get right with the Con-federacy, brother! A whole regiment of pseudo-but-ternuts have driven their limousines onto the old campground to renew the battle. Who are these gray ghosts? A phalanx of antiquarians who will never be defeated—the Sobbing Sisters, and the Confederate Songsters.

The Sobbing Sisters of Southern Secession

A fine history of this organization may be found in Mrs. Lucius H. M. Q. Finch's *History of the S.S.*,

Complete with a Roster of Regents, Vice-Regents, and Flag Bearers, and A Review of the War for Southern Righteousness, with Appendices Listing all Patriotic Duties Performed, 1868–1913.[1]

The S.S. has many impressive offices. A partial roster of these will undoubtedly be of great interest to the public.

Distinguished Grand Regent—A post of honor, usually bestowed on the hapless wife of the local State Senator.

Vice Regent—This lady handles all matters of vice which occur in the group. For such offenses as teasipping, or owning a copy of the Gettysburg Address, members may be required to turn in their lock of Robert E. Lee's hair.

Grand Flagwoman—She is in charge of caring for the half million memorial flags which drape the windows at every S.S. meeting. Other duties include periodic de-mothing of old Rebel flags.

Grand Monument Scraper—This heavy-duty national post carries the responsibility of cleaning and polishing the 526,000 Confederate monuments in the United States.

Grand Lee Bushbeater—This officer is in charge of beating the bushes for any unmarked spot where Robert E. Lee ever sat, stood, lay, or spit. This officer carries on her back an official portable granite marker.

[1] In this booklet one also learns that the S.S. is the parent organization of the Sons of Confederate Deserters.

President-General of Harassment—The chief lobbyist of the group; the post is currently held by Mrs. Gerard Lafour Swamp of Bayou Bayous, Louisiana. When she is not polishing cannonball fences on her lovely Slush Creek Plantation, Mrs. Swamp doubles as a stock car anouncer. Her official duties include speaking to businessmen's luncheons on such topics as why city hall needs another statue of Leonidas Polk.

No discussion of the S.S. would be complete without a mention of the Graylist. The Graylist is the blacklist of the Confederacy. Those on it are boycotted, bombarded with letters and telegrams, and occasionally poked with umbrellas. One may be placed on the Graylist for such offenses as:

1. Having Yankee generals on the family tree.
2. Not having Confederates on the family tree.
3. Using the term "Civil War."
4. Calling a Confederate a "Rebel."
5. Hinting that the South might have lost a battle.
6. Not liking hushpuppies.

THE CONFEDERATE WARBLER

This thrush in gray hums constantly during Civil War Centennial celebrations. The songs are tired ones—"Dixie," "Lorena," or "The Vacant Chair." Since there is little hope that the old tunes will fade away, perhaps some new lyrics might help.

DIXIE

I wish I'd been begotten,
  Somewhere besides the Land of Cotton,
Get Away, Get Away, Get Away, Dixie Land.
There's buckwheat cakes with truckstop batter,
  Phony country ham and cold egg platters,
Get Away, Get Away, Get Away, Dixie Land.

Battered Hymn of the Republic

Mine eyes have seen the Centennial till my corneas
are sore,
    I've sat on re-enactment bleachers, till my
    Rebel suit is wore.
I'm tired of hearing speeches 'bout some great Confederate bore,
    They just go on and on.

The war will never be over. Let minié balls corrode,
Confederate money crumble, and imitation battle
flags rot. As long as there is a tear-jerking poem to
be read, a droll statue to be unveiled, a cannon ball
to be unearthed, a fast buck to be made—then there
will always be a Confederacy. Grant, Sheridan, Sherman—they could whip Marse Robert Lee and Re-
treating Joe Johnston. But they will never whip that
long gray line of genealogists, antique dealers, historians, promoters, and roundtable buffs—marching
to the Gray Nirvana.

The End